YO-BZF-637

With Our Whole Broken Hearts

Copyright © 2018 by Kirsten Kramer, Melanie Curtis, and Sarah Walko

All rights reserved. This book is protected by copyright.

No part of it may be reproduced, stored in a retrieval system, or transmitted in any form by any means, electronic, mechanical, photocopying, recording or otherwise without written permission from the authors.

withourwholebrokenhearts.com

New York, NY

Printed in the United States of America

Visual design: Kirsten Kramer

kirstenkramerart.com

ISBN: 978-0998851020

WITH OUR WHOLE
BROKEN HEARTS

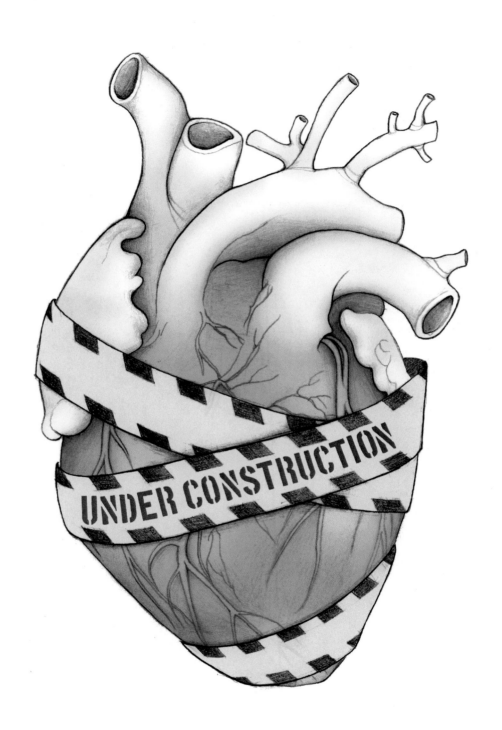

For you.

MELANIE

I thought it would work out. I had no idea how it was going to work out, and I also wasn't afraid. I was certain I needed to move forward from where I was, and I had no clue what was next. I longed for a home. For stability. In so much uncertainty, it's almost like I transcended fear and accidentally ended up in an enlightened state of complete surrender. Like, because I was so totally fucked, I was finally free to fully let go.

I ended up homeless.

I lived out of my giant office with everything I owned packed up in boxes, except my desk and the bright lights that shined on my face when I put myself out there online. I leaned my mattress up against the wall during the day and laid it down with my sleeping bag at night.

Underneath my inadvertent enlightenment and alongside the flawless comedy of extreme life breakdown, I was desperate for any kind of clarity on my future. Then... a new apartment in a new city came through. I thought this was IT. I thought a stable home was the thing I needed. What it actually led to was more loneliness, confusion and struggle.

WTF.

KIRSTEN

It was like a bomb went off, scattering all of the broken pieces of my life as far as the eye could see. I would gaze overwhelmed at the daunting heaps of destruction laid out in front of me and wonder how I would ever piece it all back together. I had to start over completely... with a child. I had to keep the ground from completely crumbling beneath us.

I had to start somewhere.

So I started to search without discouragement for the pieces I could use to rebuild. And as I sorted through the mess... as I found, piece by piece, a place to begin... I could see faintly, somewhere on the horizon, my first glimmer of hope.

SARAH

"I want to walk all night," I said to the fog.

"Why?" it asked me.

"Because now I have no direction."

I circled our house, taking various streets in the neighborhood. I arrived home again and stopped and stood on the sidewalk across the street from our apartment. The dogs were in the window, looking out into the dark, framed in the christmas lights we had hung around the plants. They couldn't see me through the darkness. I watched their heads tilting and bobbing in the light. I would have to go back in there and start all over again.

The words made me shiver and I began to walk again. I came to a field attached to an elementary school nearby our house and I stopped and sat down. I had taken the dogs there plenty of times in the daylight. Tonight it was just me and the quiet, empty, still field.

"Is my life filled with nothing now? No partner and now no direction?"

A wave of anger passed through me.

"Where's my fucking train, world?"
I said it aloud this time.

"I'm standing here. I'm standing right here. Where's the train?"

There was no response. A quiet, empty, still field. In the distance, I saw a squirrel make its way across what was to him a vast expanse of grass; a vision of open possibility.

"Am I even at a station?"

Hello friend.

Here's our story.
We are Melanie, Kirsten and Sarah.
And you are? emma♡_____
Wonderful to meet you.

Our lives blew up. Fell apart. Crumbled. Exploded. Yeah... ouch. You?

If so, we get it.

This is our spilling out and our reaching for you.
This is our laughing and crying for us both.
This is our "life is amazing" and "life is a shit show."

One thing we know from start to finish is this:
We are grateful.
We are with you.
We love you.

With Our Whole Broken Hearts.

Xoxo
M,K,S

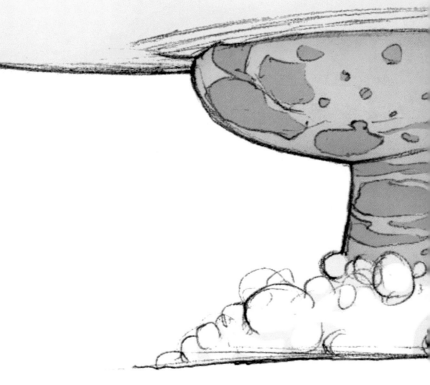

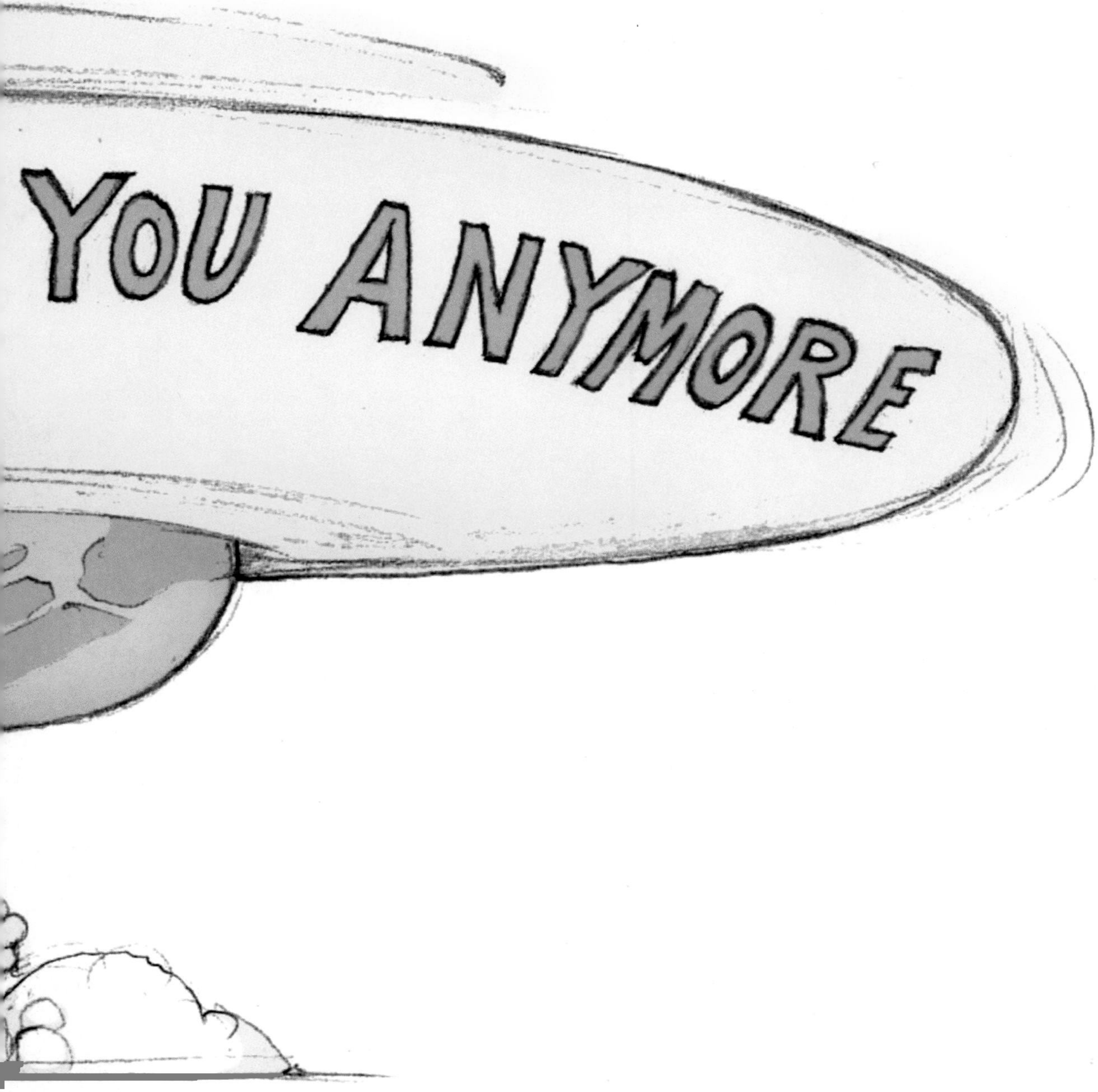
YOU ANYMORE

KIRSTEN

That first night was overwhelming. I was in shock. All I could manage was to make sure my son was ok — that he felt safe and supported by me — and to start our nightly bedtime routine. After he fell asleep in my bed, I went into the kitchen and cried. I wanted to call people and look for support, but I didn't know what to say. So I pulled out my laptop and started working on the project I was meant to be finishing for the next morning.

I spent the night awake in bed with my thoughts. All sorts of thoughts. Panic, shock, panic, panic, PANIC, shock, sadness, calm, PANIC! God! I just want to SLEEP!

I told myself, "For tonight, it's ok to stop thinking. I can think tomorrow."

And I finally slept.

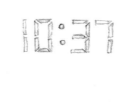

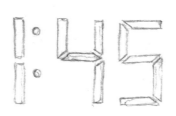

MELANIE

Three months and four days after wearing a big white puffy dress in front of 100+ friends and family in a very expensive nondescript hotel ballroom, these words entered my ears... *I don't love you anymore.*

Thinking back now, I think it's funny it was also tax day.

Shortly after the proverbial detonation of life as I knew it, I received the order of blank thank you notes meant for those 100+ people. Every note had multiple pictures of me in the big dress, dolled up for a day of dreams coming true.

Having little clarity or ability at that time on how to handle the scenario I found myself in, I proceeded to write those thank you notes in a fog of confusion, pain and fear.

I expressed legitimate gratitude for all the love and generosity those notes acknowledged, and at the same time, every single one of them felt like a lie.

YOU ANYMORE

The fantasy I didn't even know I was living in before detonation was gone, and I was writing thank you notes through the smoke.

As time went on, I would occasionally see those notes stuck up on the fridges of my friends. Each time, it felt like a lightning bolt of anxiety. I felt so embarrassed every time I saw one. As time went on further, I found the strength to ask those friends to please take those notes down off their fridges.

They were happy to.

SARAH

We submitted all of our paperwork via email and awaited her response.

Her name was Angel, and a few days later I got a text from her that simply said:

"Your new home is ready," from Angel in Summit.

"Meet me in the morning to get the keys."

I arrived at 7am the next morning. She was wearing stone-washed jeans, six-inch heels and fake eyelashes. Jersey Angel.

The day we moved in, I didn't even have a bed. I borrowed Melanie's air mattress and placed it on the floor, plugged it into the wall and blew it up, feeling accomplished and pathetic. So much had changed in my life and I felt devastated, confused and racked with anxiety that I was making all the wrong decisions. I was on an air mattress on the floor in Jersey in my late thirties. This was NOT how my life was supposed to look or feel.

Dear Universe, how will this ever be fixed?

Can you help me get through one more day?

RED
FLAGS

SARAH

There was a small voice inside my head often.
"Sarah, why does this feel so confusing?"
I ignored it over and over again.
"You are a silly small voice."
The rational brain joined in too. "This makes sense. Don't worry if it feels a little off.
Things line up. Give it time."

"Sarah?"

"Shhhhhhh."

MELANIE

That moment in the kitchen standing on the other side of the big island with the perfectly marbled granite countertop, him roasting carrots like this was his home and her casually mentioning his
uncircumcised penis.

My stomach twisted. I instantly felt literal pain in my head and chest.

I wasn't welcome here.

Every bit of my energy felt it.

Why didn't I walk out right then?

I didn't. I stayed for the whole dinner party. I stayed for another year.

I was so deep in denial, I earnestly thought I was choosing things for positive reasons.

That's how denial works. We trick ourselves into ignoring what our pain is so desperately trying to tell us. So desperately trying to help us see.

I would eventually figure it out.
I just didn't know that yet either.

So much more pain had to come first for me to get it.

Red flags are real. Our bodies tell us when to pause and look more closely. Try to listen when you feel yours. Try to use those moments to choose in directions our fear would have us ignore. Try to use those moments as opportunities for courage despite what feels like paralyzing uncertainty.

If you don't, that's ok too. Your experience and timeline is uniquely yours, and everything on it is working together to help us see into our own unique blind spots. Everything on our path is helping us learn. Grow. Heal. Everything is fuel for our ultimate reckoning, rebirth, and rise.

KIRSTEN

I was terrified.

It was the first time he had ever crossed the line and I was so shocked that he did. In the moment, I knew to call the police... but then they arrested him.

And I started to doubt myself. And make excuses in my mind for what happened. It was somehow my fault... I did something wrong to make him that angry...

Maybe it wasn't as bad as I thought it was...

I spent the night alone with my then 6-month-old son, in a panic. I got him safely and soundly to bed, and lay awake the whole night in fear of the hours and days to come. I couldn't do it on my own. I had a baby. I had no job. I was far away from home and family; all the way across the country.

His family was already blaming me as they pulled together the bail money. As they called me up to prep me for what to say to get him out of this.

I had nowhere to go and a child to worry about... who needed me to be strong and keep things safe and stable for him. So I pretended it was all ok and that things would get better.

I needed to.

THE CYCLE OF ABUSE

KIRSTEN

It was my first week of being completely on my own.

I started hearing this beeping. It was incessant.
It took me a while to figure out where it was coming from.

Every time I would hear the beep, I would try to chase it... like someone trying to find their phone when it's buzzing. But the beeping would stop as soon as I started searching, and I would have to give up. I started to think of it as a message to me... of the incredible burden on my shoulders of having to run a household completely on my own... of how deeply I could fail at this all.

After a few months, I got used to the sound of the beep... like when one lives close to a train and gets so accustomed to the sound of it passing, that they barely notice it. Of course, visitors would notice it and ask me about it. And I'd privately cringe with the reminder of what a failure I secretly felt that I was.

I finally figured out where it was coming from,
but couldn't figure out how to make it stop.

I gave in and admitted defeat... and decided to just embrace it.

It still beeps.

SARAH

I drove back from the holiday break where I had been staying with my sister. She and her husband and two kids lived in a huge beautiful four bedroom home. I looked around at our tiny rented apartment. There was a pan in the kitchen, still soaking from a few days earlier because I had scrubbed and scrubbed it but could not get the crusted remains of the sauce I had cooked out of it. The pan felt like my life in the moment — like every time I failed at getting that thing cleaned, it was a perfect illustration on how I was failing at life. I thought of my sister's kitchen. There were shiney clean pans everywhere, beautifully hung from hooks above a kitchen island with a sparkling marble top. I couldn't even clean a single, solitary pan, let alone have a normal kitchen, or a fancy one.

No wonder my life fell apart.

A few days later I went to the store and bought a new copper pan. Mel saw it when she came home and said, "You know, I was holding onto that old pan because I thought my mom would want me to, as it was hers. But she doesn't actually care." We threw it out. I cooked with the new pan and washed it out quickly and easily. Maybe I was being too hard on myself? Maybe I'm at a difficult moment, but I'm not FAILING AT LIFE like I thought I was every single time I scrubbed that old pan.

MELANIE

My Mom gave me one of her pans after I gave everything in my old house a big unenlightened middle finger.

Sometimes you just need a new pan.

REFLECTIVE
SECOND PERSON

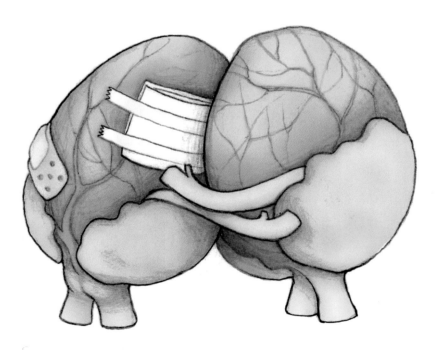

KIRSTEN

I was in my therapist's office. It was one of my first sessions with her and I was running through everything that had happened up to that point that had brought me to seek her help.

It was an intimidating path to get to my sessions with her... literally. I had to enter the large glass double doors of the massive government building, amongst the lawyers and ADAs and police officers hustling in and out of the building... to a small desk where I showed my ID to obtain an entrance badge... through a security checkpoint... up the crowded elevators... to a phone on the wall of the elevator dock, where I dialed a number to be buzzed in through another set of glass doors... to get in line to be once again identified and asked to sit in a waiting area until my therapist called on me.
I felt small and vulnerable.

I talked through all that I had suddenly lost since the *incident* a few weeks before. I was still in shock and incredibly overwhelmed. I was terrified. I talked of how much I had always feared ending up in the situation I now found myself in... that I feared being a single mom on my own. I had little confidence in myself that I could manage it all on my own.

My therapist stopped me at that moment and said, "but you're already doing it!"

I realized then that where I thought I was failing by putting so much unrealistic pressure and responsibility on myself, I was blinding myself from seeing how much I was holding things together; picking up the pieces I could salvage from the wreckage, dusting them off, and putting them into place
to rebuild.

In that bleak little government office with flourescent lighting and no windows, hearing the conversations of government staff pass back and forth down the hallway outside the door... imagining other women like me, small and vulnerable, but also strong and hopeful, sitting in the waiting area down the hall, waiting for their turn to seek help... I found my confidence and strength and hope to embrace my new path...

and embrace being on my own.

SARAH

"You look like you've been punched in the face," he said.

I half smiled. "Feel like I have."

"Do you want to talk about it?"

"Not really. What's there to talk about?"

"You just seem so sad."

"I am sad. It's been really hard. Sometimes I think, would things have been different if I had a father,
or stepfather, or anyone around who would have protected me more."

He was quiet for a long time, looking at me, then looking away and thinking.
"Well, the reality is you didn't have that. And what's the point in wondering how things could or could not have been different? The reality is, you come from a long lineage of really strong and really resilient women. It's the women in your family in both past and present who are going to get you through this. Not the protection of a man or the absence of the protection of a man. Look to the women and do as they would do, as they DO do, and as they would tell you to do. That's your protection."

MELANIE

It was night in New York City. Raining. We stood under a scaffolding. The light reflected off the wet pavement. ... I told her everything.

I felt torn. Tortured. Uncertain. In pain. So embarrassed. Ashamed.

It seemed wildly obvious given everything, that I should say I'm done. But I could not get past this idea...

"I gave my word..."

Her reply?

"There is no contract."

My friend is a hard core New York attorney. Thank god. She stood there under that scaffolding, facing me in fierce friendship and full clarity. Her confidence gave me confidence. Her strength gave me strength. Her certainty helped me find my own power to choose.

She helped me see things from a different, dispassionate perspective. She helped me understand that the integrity of my word does not bind me forever when new information is introduced thus altering an original agreement. She helped me see that the contract I had committed myself to was now void.

With that, I was free. Free from the suffocating uncertainty I had felt since tax day. Free to start even considering next steps. Free to move forward knowing my integrity was still in tact.

On this day in the dark night of New York, blasted by the light of my friend's reflection, I connected to my own power to set new boundaries and standards at any moment I decide it's time to change. I connected to my own ability to take action in conditions and feelings I could have never predicted. My mind opened and I touched my own strength in an irreversible way.

Who knew I could be this grateful for a hard core New York attorney?
I am.

ACTIVE HEALING

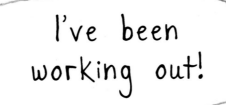

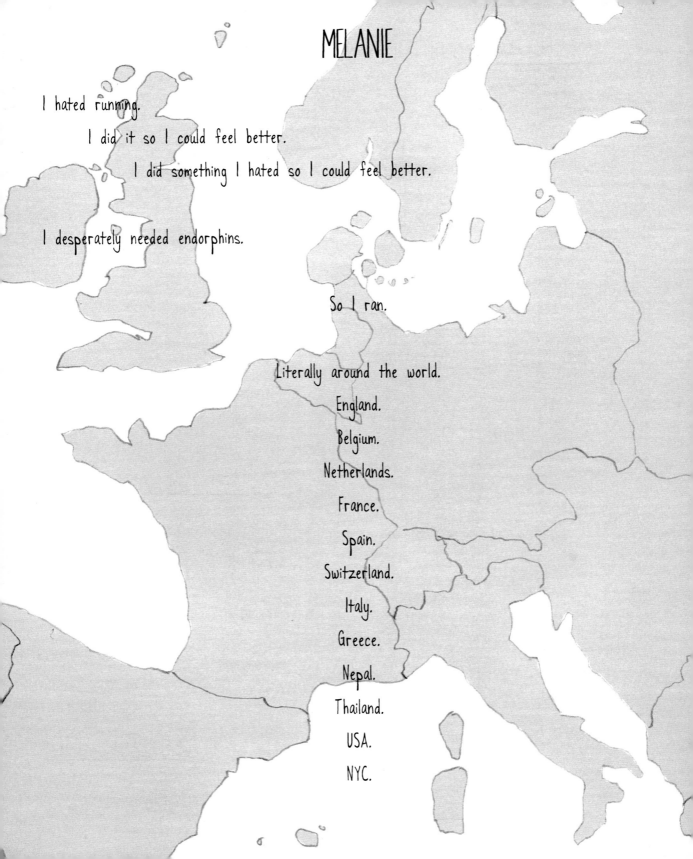

MELANIE

I hated running.

I did it so I could feel better.

I did something I hated so I could feel better.

I desperately needed endorphins.

So I ran.

Literally around the world.

England.

Belgium.

Netherlands.

France.

Spain.

Switzerland.

Italy.

Greece.

Nepal.

Thailand.

USA.

NYC.

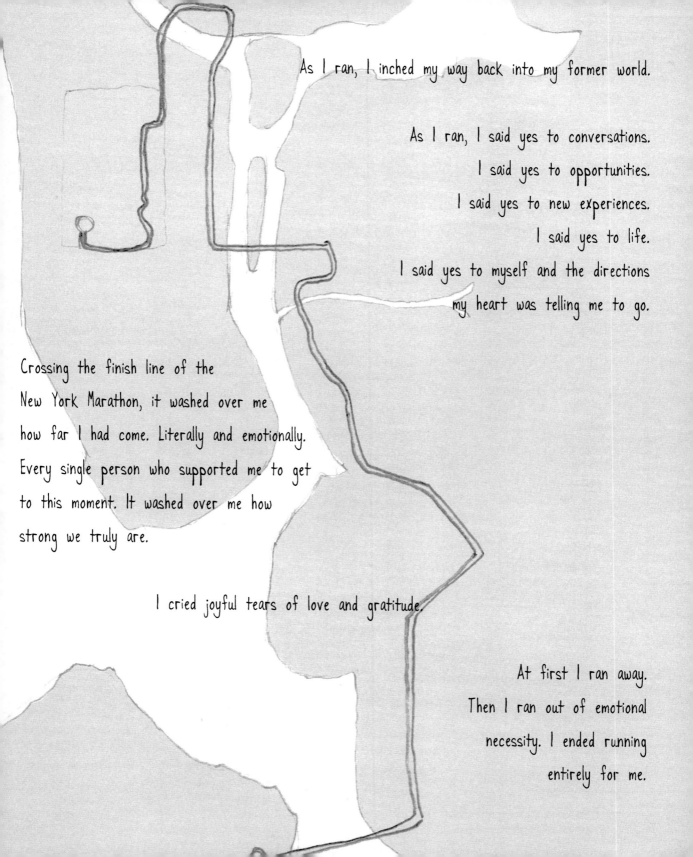

As I ran, I inched my way back into my former world.

As I ran, I said yes to conversations.
I said yes to opportunities.
I said yes to new experiences.
I said yes to life.
I said yes to myself and the directions
my heart was telling me to go.

Crossing the finish line of the
New York Marathon, it washed over me
how far I had come. Literally and emotionally.
Every single person who supported me to get
to this moment. It washed over me how
strong we truly are.

I cried joyful tears of love and gratitude.

At first I ran away.
Then I ran out of emotional
necessity. I ended running
entirely for me.

SARAH

Running was my hope and one of my forms of prayer. When it rained I ran out in it, circling the blocks of our house. I went running in the forest nearby, where I was surrounded by stunning nature; old trees next to young sprouts and new growth, all of it leaning into the light, leaning into seasons. I watched it as I ran through it; winter, death, decay, hibernation, birth, new growth. Cycles.

"Be Here Be Here Be Here," I reminded myself to remain present.

I ran to keep going. I ran to release sadness, anger and fear. I cried as I ran. I ran through the forest praying for guidance, asking my guides to run alongside of me. It was me, a little black dog and a crowd of ghost guides running and running through an ancient forest.

KIRSTEN

Synchronized swimming.

I was 38 years old when I joined this team, along with 15 other *mature* (in the loosest sense of the word) men and women who were JUST learning the sport for the first time.

Teammates. Ridiculousness. Routines. OMG, these counts are so fast! Everyone is out of sync. Everyone is laughing. Eugene just kicked Andy in the eye. Oops! I just got lifted out of the water by four people!! I feel like a superstar! Shachar is making love to the judges with his gaze... HOW DOES HE DO THAT?? I just kneed Thomas in the groin. Laughter!! #SynchroWisdom posts. Blooper videos on Facebook. Laughter!!! Training! Training! Training!

Our first big competition in Miami and I'm having panic attacks. I'm physically and mentally exhausted. Who is going to take care of my 5-yr-old while I travel across the country to do this? Where am I going to get the money for my travel?

All I can think is that if I can do this one thing... if I can get to Miami, and do the best that I can do, even if I am a total disaster... just get to Miami and compete with my team... and be able to say that despite EVERYTHING, despite all the ways in my life that I am struggling... that I DID this ONE THING!! It will all be worth it.

And I did.

And I even brought home a gold medal!

COPING EFFORTS

MELANIE

Carol said, "Sometimes you just need another heartbeat in the house."

I hit the therapist jackpot. Sometimes we need a pro and Carol was mine.

...

Even though this totally sucked... like come ON... fucking feelings. Wow... Sweet lord, the fucking feelings...
ahhhhhhhhhhh...

Geez.

Even when this, um, phase... was lasting WAY longer than I ever could have anticipated... even when I was in full WTF status, I also can't lie... there was always a part of me, deep in the unalterable center of myself, that believed... that knew...

This is all for me.

I have no clue what's awesome about this yet, but I know it is.

Even on my darkest, loneliest days, I believed the Universe had my back.

I believe it still does today.

Why? Every bit of my experience points to it being true.

...

I rescued a beautiful hilarious cat who cuddles like a champion and loves like the little lioness she is. Carol was right.. I needed her heartbeat in our house.

KIRSTEN

I went swimming in the ocean, like I would often do to calm the anxiety. There was something

peaceful about being that far away from the shore; being alone with the waves and the sea and

the sky. I went to turn around and swim back to where I had started, and the current was

so strong and the waves so choppy, I was getting slapped in the face with waves every time I

went to

take a breath and felt like I wasn't moving forward at all.

That's how the worst days feel. But they pass, and I keep going,

and I make my way forward..

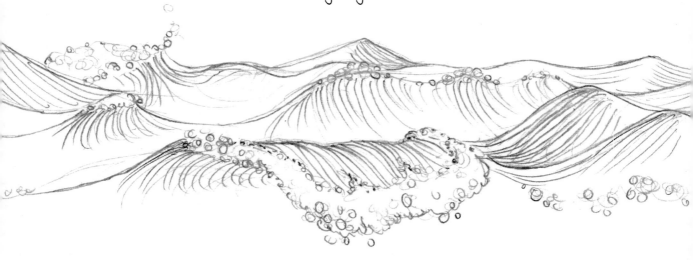

SARAH

There was a park nearby where we lived

with a small lake in the center of it.

In the springtime,

two cranes began appearing,

one white and one grey.

I began speaking to the two cranes I saw

at the lake when I went there.

I started asking them for two wishes.

They were simple; peace and love.

The grey one was peace,

the white one was love.

Hello friends, I said to them each time.

Hello peace, hello love.

SOLO MINDSET SHIFT

SARAH

Om Namah Shivaya

A five syllable mantra in Hindu mythology devoted to Lord Shiva, a meditation leading to self realization.

I planted myself on the livingroom floor to listen.

The three sections of Om means the three conditions of waking, dreaming, rest; and the three levels of cognizant, oblivious, subliminal; and in addition, the three all inclusive procedures of coming, being, and going.

Namah means devotion, praise, regard. Nothing is mine as a unique individual; everything is thine as the Absolute Reality.

Shivaya is the reality that is the ground out of which the others develop. It is that "ink," as it were, that is not separate from the numerous structures which might seem to show or be made from that ink.

In the process of self realization is this:
One comes to see that she is one and the same with the Absolute Reality.

Maybe the journey isn't so much about becoming anything. Maybe it's about un-becoming everything that isn't really you, so you can be who you were meant to be in the first place.
—Unknown

KIRSTEN

I was operating for so long in crisis mode... it was over a year, now. I would do all the things I needed to do to maintain a healthy, stable life for my son and myself... but I wasn't allowing myself to truly heal yet; to truly start inviting happiness and joy and hope back into my life. I realized I was putting up these barriers against happiness out of fear. But what was I so afraid of???

Why would I NOT want to be happy again?

It was a subtle shift on the outside, I'm sure. But I started to let myself enjoy life again... in small, little ways... baby steps. It didn't all happen at once — the shift — but gradually, things started to feel different. I started to enjoy things a little bit more. I started to open up again to friendship and love and happiness and joy. And I started to learn to leave the fears behind me whenever they came up... watching them get smaller and smaller, the further I walked away from them.

FEAR

MELANIE

I looked in the mirror and it hit me... DAMN. It hit me straight, all caps, no exclamation point.

I'm HOT.

As in, smokin' hot. Sexy. Eyes-like-saucers sexy. I say this with zero ego.

This was the moment an old limiting thought that had held me down for decades came up by the roots.

In this moment, the whole thing released. I metaphorically fell backward as it extracted fully from the dirt. In this moment, I dragged deeply ingrained unconscious rejection of my own body into the light. The moment it hit the light... it was gone.

Consciousness flooded in.

It was SO CLEAR.

Something I was so blind to for so long now seemed so radically obvious.

In this moment, I saw myself. I mean really saw myself. I stood there in a quirky Barcelona hotel room having my own Avatar moment in a fun outfit and fancy full-length mirror.

I see you.

...

This is only one mindset shift of many I had on my road to full and fortified self love.

Every time I felt fear, anxiety, loneliness, hurt, etc... I used it as my guide. Equally, every time I felt joy, peace, fulfillment, freedom, connection, hilarity, love, etc... I used those as my guides too. Every feeling was pointing me to invaluable breakthroughs and new directions. Doors through which I could transform...

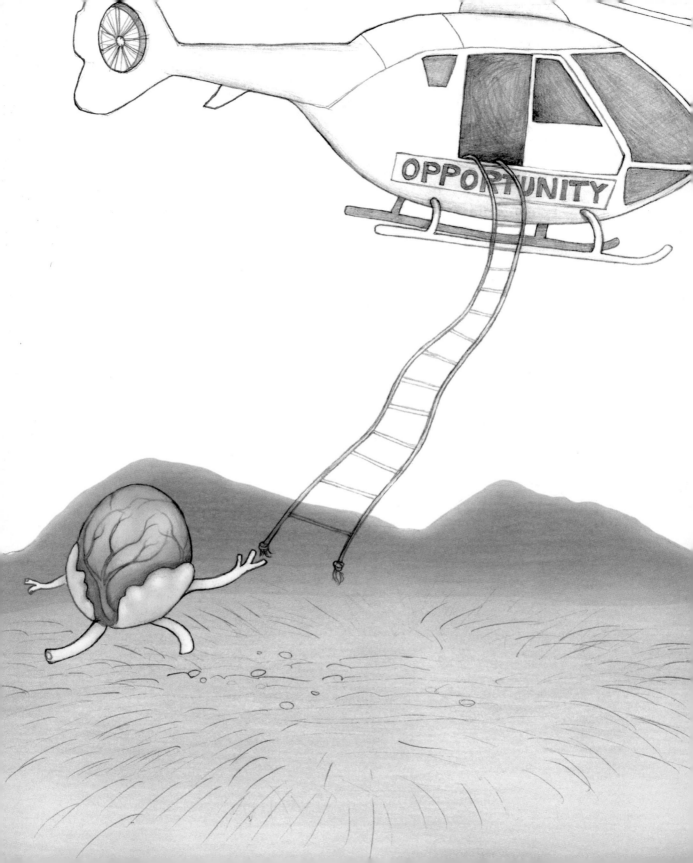

DOORS
OPENING

SARAH

"We'd like to offer you the position," she said as she sipped her coffee. I felt something jump inside me. It was less than a month since I quit my job and I was beginning to worry about what I would move on to, and how long it would take. I shook my head and finished the offer interview, telling her I would get back to her within a few days. I exited the coffee shop and walked the two blocks back to the apartment, imagining that neighborhood where the museum was, the little town that surrounded it. I knew immediately I would take the job and move there. I needed a new job and I needed to move. Two doors I needed to open, just opened. It felt sudden and scary but I had to jump and the universe was offering it to me very clearly.

MELANIE

Sooooo... how would you like to move with me to New Jersey?

Fuuuuuuuck yesssssssss!!!! I am 100% DEFINITELY IN, sight unseen, fuck yeah Jersey, NYC, nothing could stop me from doing this, nothiiiiiiiiiiiiiiiiiiiiiig!!!!! Thank fucking hell, Universe, YES!!!! This is so happening.

Sounds like it has potential... I will go check it out, and we can decide from there.

KIRSTEN

Sarah said to me,

"I think we should do a graphic memoir... about our experiences.

I think it's something your talents would be perfect for."

I was so far from ever believing I could do something like that... to step so far out of my

comfort zone of experience and knowledge. I wasn't an illustrator. I had NO experience.

And I certainly wasn't a writer!

But she was so certain.

And I trusted and believed her.

So I said, "OK!"

And we got started. Sarah, Melanie and I.

And I started to build my life in a way that would allow me to work on this project for the

next year.

And I KNEW I was working on something REAL.

I was working with two real phenomenal women.

GRATITUDE FOR THE DESTRUCTION

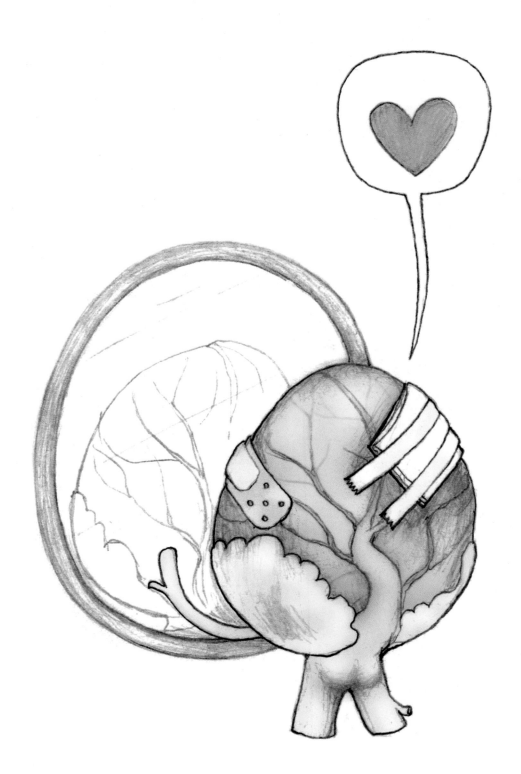

SARAH

Dear universe,

I am breaking open to who I need to be for the next chapter of my life.

I am standing next to the smoldering forest

after the fire has gone out,

knowing the heat

unleashed seeds

everywhere.

I ask you to send softness,

peace, healing, and rooted steadiness.

Maybe a walking stick that I can lean into.

Thank you old chapter for everything you have taught me.

Thank you pain, grief and trauma for all the wisdom in your storms and for the calm that is here.

Thank you for the rainbows that are coming.

Thank you life for my sacred path that is mine and mine alone and always sacred, even in the depths of the darkness.

Thank you life force for the transformation of my pain into my power.

Ruins, for me, are the beginning.

With the debris, you can construct new ideas.

They are symbols of a beginning.

– Anselm Kiefer

MELANIE

My life and identity blowing up into 18 million smithereens? Taking multiple years to be pieced back together into something that looks kind of the same but is in fact entirely new and intensely more beautiful than it ever could have been chasing mythical "perfection?"

Oh fuck yes.

Thank God.

I am no longer a cookie-cutter shell of a person buying into beliefs I didn't even know I bought in the first place. I am no longer a person blindly and intensely achieving thinking it will equate love and safety.

Now I have street cred. Now I see.

Everything I knew, believed and trusted collapsed around me and in me. Not only did I live to tell the tale, I'm telling you...

THANK GOD.

Only through the agony of massive breakdown... through the uninvited and intentional teardown of my life and identity bare to its bones could I have gotten here.

Right here. Clear. Calm. In this moment. Connected with myself and with life.

Only getting all the way to the bottom, could I begin to ricochet. To rebuild. To rise. Only actual bottom gives us a solid foundation to start over on stable ground. The stability I was yearning for I found there. And from there, I got to decide who I really wanted to be, and what that person did with her life.

I gathered my grit, my guts and I got to putting all those jagged pieces back together.

Over time they started to stick. Over time they started to take shape into something significant. Something sustainable. Substantial. Stunning. Strong.

Only through this process did I come to deeply get how critical, simple and essential it is to accept myself fully. I learned that when it came to setting my standards.. when it came to sticking to them.. when it came to navigating conflict.. when it came to standing up for myself.. and even when it came to feeling safe and happy on any old day... I learned that self-acceptance... self-love... was non-negotiable. This was the place I put my courage. Only in my commitment to growing in this single skill have I found freedom from fear, anxiety and disconnection.

I only got any of this because all my shit burned to the ground.

...

I believe our most pure, authentically expressed state.. mess and might.. is the most beautiful thing there is. Like you, I am a walking masterpiece with my chaos of color, asymmetrical edges and all-in courage. Even on the days I wear my glasses and don't brush my hair. Even on the days I rock the red dress and red lips on the red carpet. All that and everything in between is beautiful because it's me... Because it's you.

KIRSTEN

What do they say?

Clean slate?

Blank canvas?

I feel like I painted over my canvas with fresh paint.
I can still see the lumps underneath of a life lived before.

I don't want to completely erase that.

Those lumps give character to the
new story I get to paint.

OUR WORK
AS
OUR ROCK

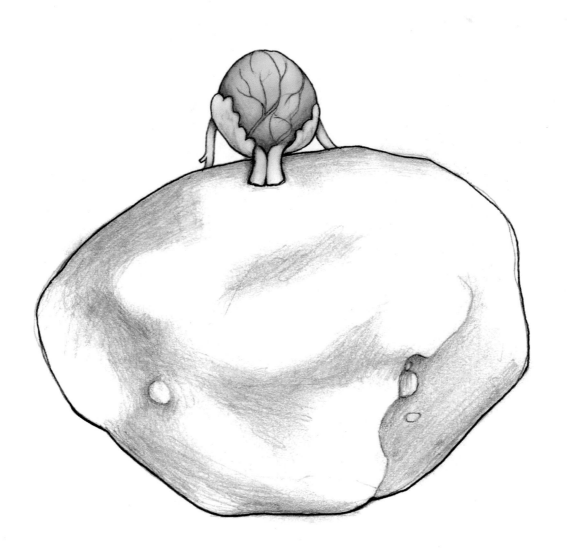

MELANIE

The best way to find yourself is to lose yourself in service of others. —Mahatma Gandhi

KIRSTEN

I do the "work" every day.

Getting out of bed, when I just want to hide away and avoid the day.

Going to the gym, when I want to sit on the couch and feel sorry for myself.

Letting go of that new guy who seems to be really sweet and awesome,

but something doesn't quite feel right about him.

Making the effort to make plans and spend time with friends, instead of wishing

they would reach out to ME more often.

Working on my creative projects to keep me moving forward on the path I want to be on.

Letting go of the fears.

The fear of being all alone.

The fear of failing.

The fear of succeeding and feeling like an imposter... a fraud.

The more I do this "work" and practice these skills, the better I get at them.

SARAH

Throughout it all, no matter how intense the pain was and sometimes because the pain was so intense, I could still walk into the studio and make work. When working on sculptures, I experimented with materials and new ways of working with ideas I had, but I was also listening. I felt the moment when my small personal narrative dissolved, slipped out the door and I was no longer my story. My body relaxed, releasing me from the story steeped in personal challenges, failures, fear and pain. I reconnected with the vastness of living, of the universe, how I was here for one blink of a second. I reconnected with our connection with each other, and loneliness left the room too. Ancient alchemists believed that you could not transform a material within your hands without transforming yourself. When I left the studio I always felt I had spent time releasing myself from the grip of my challenges and let myself be of service to the world in the best way I knew how, using the imagination in the act of creation.

I felt different when I left.

You cannot transform materials in your hands without some transformation of self.

Head to heart to hand to hope...

THE MEDICINE
IS ALWAYS
DIFFERENT

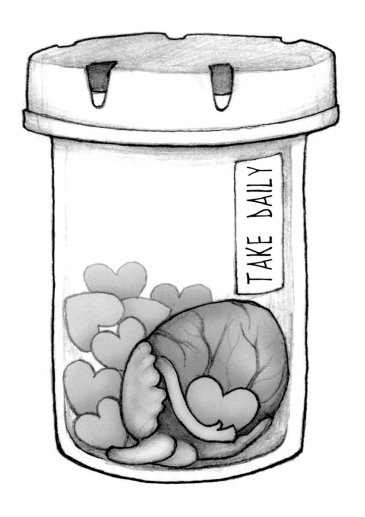

MELANIE

Penn Station waiting for my late train, jamming to a new song in my earbuds after dance class, a cool guy stops, compliments my shoes, asks me where I got them, tells me to fuck off when I tell him I got them at Target for 8 bucks on the clearance rack. I tell him I will not fuck off, it's true and I've worn them around the world. No fucking way. Yes fucking way. As he walks away to his train, he says...

"So not only are you sexy, you're also thrifty."

Correct.

I fucking love New York.

SARAH

Every single time, I thought I needed a good night's sleep.

But actually I needed:

✓ Back-to-Back Elizabethen-era films with chips and salsa.

✓ To stay up way too late reading a good book.

✓ A trip to the city to see a play, even if it wasn't that good

✓ Copious amounts of hummus and pita.

✓ To wrestle with the dogs for an hour.

✓ A completely nonstop full busy day at work so I forget my own narrative. Again.

✓ To help someone struggling more than me.

✓ To help someone struggling more than me.

✓ To help someone struggling more than me.

KIRSTEN

Binge-watching Gilmore Girls over and over and over and over and over and over and over and over and over and over...

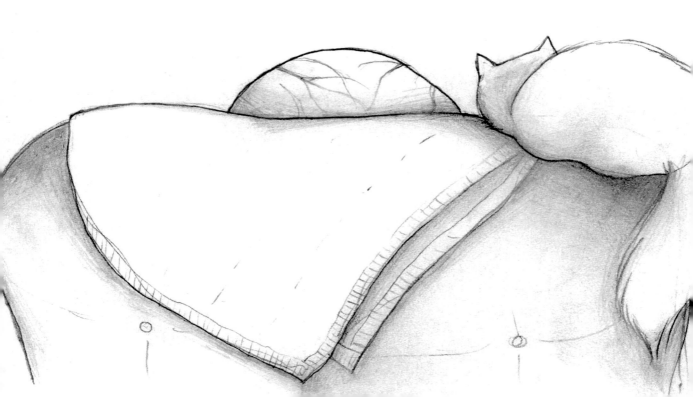

PHOENIX RISING

MELANIE

"She once believed that the damage to her mind and heart was permanent, until she met wisdom, who taught her that no pain or wound is eternal, that all can be healed, and that love can grow even in the toughest parts of her being."
-Yung Pueblo

We think a lot of things that aren't true.

I went to a friendly working dinner party where we did a simple sharing exercise. I was excited and made a comment acknowledging my even-higher-than-normal high energy, saying something like, "I'm feeling really positive this week..." To which, one of my friends immediately replied, "When are you NOT feeling positive?"

Literally everyone in the room laughed.

They laughed in recognition of my perceptibly unwavering energy and positivity in their experience of me. Like, dang, girl, you a weirdo, but I dig it 'cause obviously it's real even though I have no clue how you do it and you're probably an alien.

Totally.

I take their laughs as a high compliment. I take them as clear acknowledgment for exactly what this quote points to. To the ease and clarity I have earned only because I did the deep work slogging through my suffering. I know how confusing and irrevocable the pain feels when the wounds of our hearts are still open... when we are in the process of our egos and ideologies being stripped away, making us feel raw and ridiculously vulnerable. I take their laughs as recognition of my rising, fundamentally fueled by the deeper understanding that no pain or wound is eternal, and that we can transform any pain into so much more light and positive power.

I felt championed by these friends reflecting my impact, influence and radiance back to me in my most favorite style... an exquisitely timed, on-point joke.

Life... funny because it's true.

I was definitely welcome in this room.

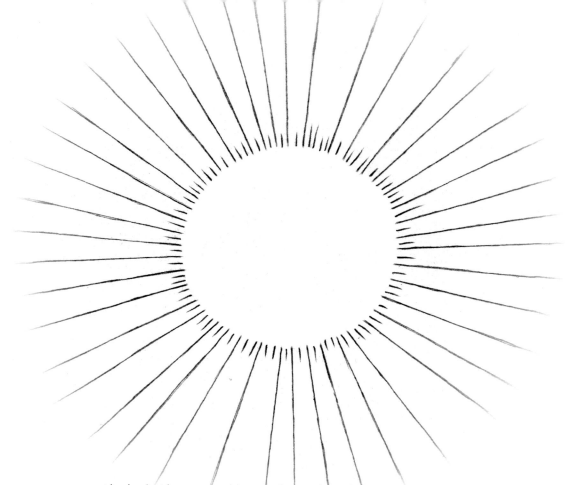

We heal. We grow. We transform through our experiences.
We come out stronger, sexier and more secure in ourselves than we ever thought possible before.
We come out loving ourselves so much that outside circumstances and others' opinions no longer
affect our stability. We source our safety and certainty inside no matter what roller coaster we
ride next. We are ready. We are capable and we know it. Because we know ourselves. Because
we have learned to trust ourselves again. To trust life. To trust that everything is for us.
That everything has positive value. Even when we can't see it, we know it's there. Even when it
takes a seemingly really really long time to see. We practice patience knowing our breakthrough
is always there with any pain or joy we feel. We rest easy in our task to simply keep looking.
With courage. With love. With delight. Delighted knowing whatever we find is another key to our
freedom. Another key to our highest self. Another key to our deepest connections. Another key
to fun that seems like it shouldn't be allowed, but it is.
Another key to the richest love we absolutely believe is possible
because we are beginning to experience exactly that.

SARAH

You don't become whole by being surrounded by light. You become whole by making darkness conscious.

The world is three days; as for yesterday, it has vanished, along with all that was in it. As for tomorrow, you may never see it. As for today, it is yours, so work in it. — Hasan al-Basri

The world is three days. Be in it. Work in it. Become whole. Open up to the pain, the cracks in the jar. It becomes fertilizer for the soil. The injury once healed becomes the soil for the great oak tree to grow and assist you in your service to the world.

If I can stop one heart from breaking,
I shall not live in vain;
If I can ease one life the aching,
Or cool one pain,
Or help one fainting robin
Unto his nest again,
I shall not live in vain.
— Emily Dickinson

KIRSTEN

When I was a little girl, I remember having moments when I would look at my hands or legs or fingers or arms, and feel like I could almost SEE myself growing... thinking to myself, "my hands are so much bigger than they used to be, and one day they will be as big as my mommy's."

I have had so many moments like that during my journey through this experience of healing and learning and growing.

I can SEE my growth as it is happening.

I have my own path waiting for me once I am done growing... or maybe I'm never done growing.

Either way, I'm figuring it out...

with my whole broken heart.

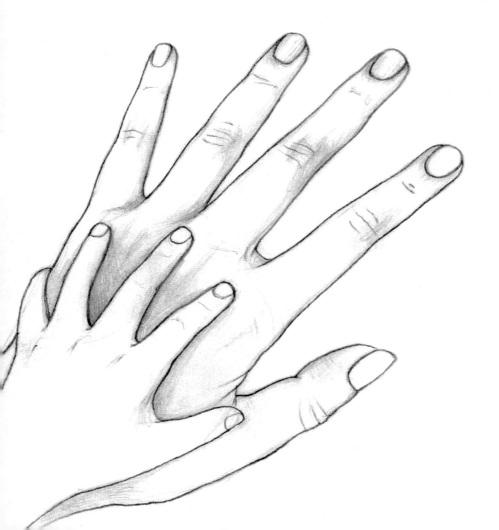

We do always figure it out, don't we?

If you're not sure, rest easy, lovely friend... your rising is coming too.

The pain and struggle is the soil from which we grow. The experience is the door through which we transform.

Trust this process.

Trust the journey.

Trust yourself.

Breathe.

Let go.

Let your heart break open.

With you all the way.

XOXO

M, K, S

PERSONAL REFLECTION

PERSONAL REFLECTION

PERSONAL REFLECTION

PERSONAL REFLECTION

PERSONAL REFLECTION

WITH OUR WHOLE BROKEN HEARTS

Melanie Curtis is a comically authentic keynote speaker, writer, and life coach (melaniecurtis.com). A Middlebury College and iPec Coaching graduate, Melanie has competed, coached and led large events around the world as a headlining professional skydiver with over 11,000 jumps to date. She has built a strong and supportive community over the last 20 years, leading and inspiring others through her message, example and positive energy. Melanie has been featured in Fast Company, on countless podcasts, and now also co-hosts her own growth-minded, spiritually seeking show, Trust the Journey (trustthejourney.today). Melanie believes love and hilarity are the two most important things in life, in that order. And we believe that too.

Sarah Walko is a visual artist, writer, director and curator and has a BA in studio art practices from the University of Maryland and an MFA from Savannah College of Art and Design (www.sarahwalko.com). For the past twelve years she has directed and curated for institutions, non-profits and independent projects and she is currently the Director of Education and Community Outreach at the Visual Art Center of New Jersey. In these various positions, as well as in everything she does, she believes in art not as a thing, but as a WAY. And we believe that too.

Kirsten Kramer is a figurative artist originating from the artist community of DUMBO in Brooklyn, NY (kirstenkramerart.com). She developed her interest in figurative work while studying Fine Art at SUNY University of Buffalo. Her work has been displayed in various group and solo exhibitions throughout the US. Her series "Hearts" in her paintings and drawings inspired the heart character in this book. She believes the heart is a symbol of so much more than comfort and connection, but of love, life and death. And we believe that too.

Made in the USA
Middletown, DE
25 June 2021

43128794R00058